Handl

'There are few stage authors writing more interestingly than Mark Ravenhill ... He is – it is now yet more evident – a searing, intelligent, disturbing sociologist with a talent for satirical dialogue and a flair for sexual sensationalism'
Financial Times

'There is an alchemy at work here which testifies to Ravenhill's talent' *Observer*

'Challenging, truthful and gripplingly dramatic, this is the stuff of theatrical benchmarks' *What's On*

Mark Ravenhill's first full-length play, *Shopping and Fucking,* was produced by Out of Joint and the Royal Court Theatre and opened at the Ambassadors Theatre prior to a national tour. It transferred to the West End in June 1997 and went on to tour internationally. His second play, *Faust,* was produced by Actors Touring Company in 1997. In 1998 Paines Plough produced *Sleeping Around*; a collaboration with Hilary Fannin, Stephen Greenhorn and Abi Morgan.

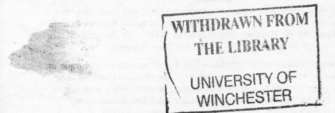

Published by Methuen in 1998

1 3 5 7 9 10 8 6 4 2

First published in the United Kingdom in 1998 by
Methuen Publishing Limited
20 Vauxhall Bridge Road, London SW1V 2SA

Random House Australia (Pty) Limited
20 Alfred Street, Milsons Point, Sydney, New South Wales 2061, Australia
Random House New Zealand Limited
18 Poland Road, Glenfield, Auckland 10, New Zealand
Random House South Africa (Pty) Limited
Endulini, 5A Jubilee Road, Parktown 2193, South Africa

Methuen Publishing Limited Reg. No. 3543167

A CIP catalogue record for this book
is available from the British Library

ISBN 0 413 73760 8

Typeset by Deltatype Ltd, Birkenhead, Merseyside
Printed and bound in Great Britain by
Cox & Wyman Ltd, Reading, Berkshire

Caution

HANDBAG

Mark Ravenhill

Methuen Drama

Handbag, commissioned by Actors Touring Company, was first performed at the Lyric Hammersmith Studio, London, on 14 September 1998. The cast was as follows:

Tom/Cardew	Tim Crouch
Lorraine/Prism	Faith Flint
Phil	Paul Rattray
Suzanne/Constance	Julie Riley
Mauretta/Augusta	Celia Robertson
David/Moncrieff	Andrew Scarborough

Directed by Nick Philippou
Designed by Gideon Davey
Lighting by Simon Mills
Sound by Christopher Shutt
Produced by Hetty Shand

Characters

Mauretta
Suzanne
David
Tom
Phil
Lorraine

Prism
Augusta
Cardew
Moncrieff
Constance

The first production of the play doubled the characters as follows: **Mauretta–Augusta**, **Suzanne–Constance**, **David–Moncrieff**, **Tom–Cardew**, **Lorraine–Prism**.

A slash in the dialogue (/) is a cue for the next actor to start their line, creating overlapping dialogue.

Scene One

Suzanne, **Mauretta** *and* **David** *waiting*.

Mauretta I hope he's alright.

Suzanne It's probably just a bit difficult . . . performing . . . to order.

David It means a lot to Tom. It means a lot to both of us.

Mauretta To all of us.

David And when it means so much . . . to all of us . . . then it must be difficult to have a wank.

Suzanne . . . A wank?

David Alright. It must be hard to spill your love seed. / Summon up the spirits of the ancestors of fertility.

Suzanne I'm not saying . . . no. Just wank's a bit . . . functional.

David Alright.

Pause.

Mauretta If Tom's finding it a bit difficult . . .

David He'll be fine.

Mauretta Yes, but if the pressure's really / blocking . . .

David He'll get there.

Mauretta Then maybe you / should . . .

David No. We agreed. This is Tom's . . . I mean, I'm right behind Tom . . . but Tom really wants to . . . I mean, no kid wants to end up with my gene pool.

Mauretta You shouldn't be so / down on yourself.

David Gene swamp, really. I'm still trying to sort myself out. Tom's more . . . sorted.

Pause.

Mauretta Maybe we can help him.

Suzanne A helping hand?

Mauretta Well, I think that's David's territory.

David I'll give it a go.

Mauretta I mean ... I don't know. Music or something.

David I know, I know.

David *produces a porn magazine.*

David This should do the trick.

Suzanne No.

David Might get him going.

Suzanne No. No.

Mauretta If it does / the trick ...

Suzanne I'm not having my ... our baby is not being / conceived with some oiled up, fake tanned rent-a-dick porn model. I'm not having that.

David (*showing different pages*) This one? This one? Or ... how about? (*Porn star voice.*) Hey Brad, my parents are away for the summer. How about / coming over and having a kid?

Suzanne Put it away. Put it away.

Beat.

Mauretta Go on. Give it a go.

Suzanne Yes?

Mauretta Yeah. Go on. If that's what it takes ...

David Alright. (*Porn star voice.*) Oh Brad, yeah. Give me that baby. Give it to me.

Exit **David** *with porn.*

Suzanne I thought you wouldn't want ...

Mauretta Anything that works. Just waiting for the
starter's orders now. My body's ready now, you know? All
those little hormones rushing around screaming . . . come
on, come on. We're up for it. Start the clock.

Suzanne It's gonna work.

Mauretta Think so?

Suzanne I know it is.

Mauretta How?

Suzanne I dunno. I just . . . believe. I love you.

Mauretta I love you.

Suzanne Mummy.

Mauretta Mummy.

Enter **David** *and* **Tom**.

Mauretta How did you . . . ?

Tom *holds up a cup.*

Tom Ta-tum. All done.

David Got there all by himself.

Suzanne Well done.

They all hug and kiss **Tom**. **Tom** *gives the cup to* **Mauretta**.

Mauretta When I was a kid my dad walked out. One
day he came home and he packed a bag and he stuck his
head round the door and he said: 'I'm going out'. And that
was it. He was gone and we never mentioned him again.
But people would look at you and they'd say: 'It's not
right. A mum and a dad's best for a kid. A kid's gotta have
a mum and a dad.'
So they should be fucking pleased now. Because you my
child will be doubly blessed. There's a positive glut of
parents here for you. You've enough mummies and daddies
that if one decides to pack a bag and move on you've got
plenty to be going on with.

And we love you and we want you and we're waiting for you.

Mauretta *kisses the cup, passes it around the others who each kiss the cup. Loud music through the walls.*

Suzanne Oh god. The child abuser.

Tom Yes?

Suzanne Next door. The child abuser. We reckon he's got all the local kids in there. Chopped up.

Tom No?

Suzanne And we reckon he turns the music up really loud so you can't hear the screams.

Tom Oh.

David Joke.

Suzanne Yes. It's a joke.

Mauretta Right then.

Suzanne Right then. Here we go.

Mauretta Can't let this get cold.

Suzanne Fingers crossed.

Suzanne *kisses* **Mauretta**. *Exit* **Suzanne** *and* **Mauretta**.

Tom It's really not very conducive. Boom boom boom. What's that? (*The porn.*)

David That? Doesn't matter.

Tom Show me. Oh. Why did you . . . ?

David Just thought you might need . . .

Tom Not with that.

David Alright.

Tom No. I don't want this to be . . . that's . . . it's sordid.

David Sorry.

Tom . . . Sorry. I just want everything to be . . . You see so many kids. At the end of school, the parents come and pick them up. And I watch them from the staffroom window, and they grab hold of the kid's hand and it's: 'shut up' – swipe – 'keep your fucking mouth shut'. I mean, how's a child supposed to grow, develop and grow, when there's so much anger and, and . . . ugliness? And that's why I want . . . We can do so much better than that. We can create something calm and positive. We can do that.

Pause.

David I love you.

Tom And . . . I love you. Daddy.

David Daddy.

Scene Two

Victoria Station.

Prism, *in great distress, is searching. She carries a suitcase.*

Prism Oh . . . where? Oh where can it be?

Enter **Augusta**, *carrying a large handbag.*

Prism Oh thank god.
(*To* **Augusta**.) Excuse me. Excuse me. You've made a terrible mistake.

Augusta I don't think so.

Prism But you have.

Augusta I never make mistakes.

Prism Please – there has been an awful muddle.

Augusta Let me pass.

Prism We must sort out this confusion.

Augusta Are you a lunatic?

Prism I am a novelist.

Augusta That is much the same thing.

Prism No.

Prism *grabs the handbag.*

Augusta Let go of my bag.

Prism It's not your bag.

Augusta I was warned that London would be like this. Lunatics, / brigands, vagabonds.

Prism It's not your bag. It is my bag. This ... This is your bag.

Augusta Oh. Are you sure?

Prism Quite sure.

Augusta How can you tell?

Prism Because they are quite different. Look. Look.

Augusta I'm afraid looking is not one of my natural talents.

Prism But surely you / can see ... ?

Augusta In fact all my talents are quite artificial. I shall use my glasses. Oh. What is this?

Prism It is a handbag.

Augusta A handbag?

Augusta *drops the bag.*

Prism Don't. No. Don't. / Take care.

Augusta An ordinary handbag.

Prism If you have caused any / damage –

Augusta The most ordinary handbag I have ever seen.

Prism How superficial you are. You must think of the inside. What is inside is of great importance.

Augusta To challenge substance over style is quite a challenge to society is it not?

Prism (*talking into bag*) There. There. No damage done. You are quite alright.

Augusta Whatever are you . . . ?

Prism The manuscript of my new novel.

Augusta You are rather plain to be a novelist are you not?

Prism I don't think you should call me plain. Plain is a rather insulting word to use with someone you don't know.

Augusta What an eejit . . . foolish person I am. I was forgetting one of the primary rules of life: insult only those to whom you have been introduced. Miss O'Flaherty.

Prism Miss Prism.

Augusta Prism. That is rather scientific, is it not?

Prism O'Flaherty. That is rather Irish is it not?

Augusta Pray, don't talk to me about Ireland. I detest Ireland.

Prism But you are Irish.

Augusta Oh there are very few Irish left nowadays on account of their choosing to die in such vast numbers. If one encounters famine, they all must.

Prism You sound Irish.

Augusta How persistent you are. I am not Irish. Except by birth and upbringing. Which, I am sure you will agree, are of no relevance whatsoever. O'Flaherty does make me sound a little Irish but I shall lose the name O'Flaherty very soon. I shall be married before the season is quite over.

Prism You seem very certain of that.

Augusta It is inevitable. I am in my full bloom. I am

here to live with my sister and her husband. No doubt you have heard of them. The Moncrieffs.

Prism   Colonel Moncrieff?

Augusta   There. I knew you had.

Prism   Colonel Moncrieff of Belgrave Square?

Augusta   I believe his Indian campaign was much remarked upon. To lose so many men in such a short space of time always leads to comment and medals and so forth. Yes. Colonel Moncrieff of Belgrave Square.

Prism   Then we are making the same journey. I too am going to live with Colonel and Mrs Moncrieff of Belgrave Square.

Augusta   How remarkable. No doubt you are a distant relation of the Colonel's. Oh, sister, delighted, delighted.

Prism   No, not sister. I am to be nanny to your sister's child.

Augusta   Oh. It is born?

Prism   No. But it is imminent.

Augusta   A nanny? Didn't you a moment ago tell me that you were a novelist?

Prism   I am a novelist . . . and a nanny.

Augusta   That doesn't seem quite proper. A baby and a book. That could lead to great confusion could it not?

Prism   It could not. I am never confused.

Augusta   I am not quite sure it is proper to talk to a nanny. Particularly such a very plain one.

Prism   Plain, plain, plain. You are quite intolerable.

Augusta   You understand me already. Now come. I like you a great deal and as I like you a great deal, you may carry my bag.

Scene Three

Office.

Phil *stands. Blood is running from his nose.*

Phil   Fuck. Fuck. Fuck.

Enter **David** *with bowl of water and cloth.*

David   Alright. If you . . .

Phil   Cunt. Cunt. Cunt.

David   If you sit down.

Phil   Fucking cunt.

David   Alright. If you sit down so I can . . .

Phil   Ooooh.

David   It's not so bad. Looks a lot worse than it is.

Phil   It's not safe is it? Nowhere's safe when some cunt can just leap at you and . . .

David   Keep still. Almost there.
There. No serious damage done.

Phil   Should have been police around.

David   Well . . .

Phil   Should be police everywhere with cunts around like that. They should have cameras up. Watching them.

David   Maybe it's just as well they didn't.

Phil   They want to get that cunt on video. That's what they want to do.

David   You think so? Could be tricky. Put cameras up and you get all sorts of other cunts on video as well.

Phil   Well yeah . . .

David   Like cunts who snatch handbags from other poor unsuspecting cunts.

Phil What you saying?

David Nothing.

Phil Come on. What you saying?

David I'm saying that maybe there's a reason why you got a bloody nose.

Phil You reckon?

David And maybe if you snatch a handbag it's not surprising if someone runs after you and gives you a hard time.

Phil I gave it back.

David Wise move. He might have carried on kicking if you hadn't.

Phil I could have handled him.

David Of course you could.

Phil You Old Bill?

David No.

Phil You gonna grass me up?

David No.

Phil So what you after?

David Me? Nothing. Just . . . a good Samaritan.

Phil You work here?

David That's right.

Phil You'll be in trouble. Back here after hours.

David Oooh, I think they'll forgive me. Drink?

Phil I've gotta go.

David Stay for a drink. I'll raid the boardroom. Glass of wine? Beer?

Phil Alright. Beer.

Exit **David**. **Phil** *goes over to a TV/Video. Pushes play. Video starts:*

Suzanne (*on video*)   And that tea. Is that your regular brand of tea?

Lorraine (*on video*)   Oh yeah. We always have this one.

Suzanne (*on video*)   And why do you think that is Lorraine?

Lorraine (*on video*)   I don't know. It's a family thing.

Suzanne (*on video*)   Is that an important consideration when you're shopping?

Lorraine (*on video*)   You get a taste for things don't you?

Enter **David** *with two cans of beer.*

Suzanne (*on video*)   So, you wouldn't say you often try new products?

Lorraine (*on video*)   Do you think I'm old fashioned?

David   Drinks are served.
You enjoying that?

Phil   Is that your job?

David   A part of it.

Phil   Ask people about tea bags?

David   Right now, we're the most sought after team in the business.

Phil   To ask people about tea bags?

David   To ask people about tea bags ... in a completely new way. We actually go and live with the consumers of tea bags. Tea bags and air fresheners and pizzas. The full gamut of modern life. Live with them for a week, take along a video camera and video their choices, their habits and discover all the stuff statistics never tell us. Yeah. Thought you'd be impressed.

Phil   Live with them?

David   Live with them.

Phil   Could get a bit . . .

David   Strictly impersonal. Observation not relationship orientated.

Phil   Still, you must think about . . . I mean, she's (*Woman on video.*) . . . she's alright, isn't she?

David . Not my type.

Phil   No. What's your type?

David   Well . . .

Phil   Bet your type's more . . .

David   Yes?

Phil   Bet I'm more your type.

David   What makes you think that?

Phil   'Cos you're a good Samaritan with a stiffy.

David   Well . . . yes.

Phil   Good Samaritan. He didn't walk by. That's the one, isn't it? Didn't walk by. Got involved.

Phil *kneels down, undoes* **David***'s flies. Sucks* **David***'s cock. Almost instantly,* **David***'s pager goes off.*

Phil   Fucking hell. What's that?

David   Pager.

Phil   I thought you were alarmed.

David   Listen . . . I've got to go.

Phil   Tea bag emergency?

David   Come on. I've got to go.

Phil   I'll finish you off.

David   No.

Phil   Can't go until I've finished you off.

David It's really very important. I . . .

Phil Only take a few minutes.

Phil *unclips the pager from* **David***'s trousers, sets it down some distance away from them, then unzips* **David***'s flies and starts sucking him off again. This goes on for some time. The pager beeps.* **David** *tries to move but* **Phil** *holds him in place. More sucking. The pager is still beeping.* **David** *struggles to get to it.* **Phil** *gets there first.*

Phil Don't let it control you.

David Please.

Phil Be your own person. Say: this is my time and I am my own person.

David Come on.

Phil *reads the page.*

Phil 'Labour started'?

David That's right.

Phil What does that mean? Labour started?

David It means . . . it means my child is about to be born.

Phil Yeah? Poof with a kid. Wicked.

David So. Yeah, wicked. I ought to / go to the hospital.

Phil I wasn't there. My kid was born. I wasn't there. Her mother was in another hostel. They never told me. She should have told me but she's a junkie cunt.

David Did you want to be there?

Phil Best to keep away. Do you want to be there?

David Yes.

Phil I can't even take care of myself. I can't work it out. There's so much to do isn't there? You've got to clean yourself, your clothes, your room. You've gotta buy things

and pay for things and order things. All this stuff just to
take care of yourself. I mean, I can't see how anyone does
it. I just can't cope. How do you cope?

David   I don't know. It's just natural.

Phil   For you. Yes. For people like you. But for me . . . I
mean I cut myself. In the bathroom or the kitchen or
whatever. All the time these little cuts. And I look down at
it, at the blood and that and I think: I should do something
about this. I should . . . it should be natural to know what
to do. But I can't remember or maybe I never knew. So I
just stand there. Watch myself bleeding.

David   Sort yourself out.

Phil   I'm trying you know. I try. But things just keep on
fucking up.

David   Then try harder.

Phil   I wet myself. I wet the bed. Every night I wake
myself up with it and I don't know what to do and I lie in
it.

David   That's disgusting.

Phil   I know.

David   Get a doctor. Get a social worker.

Phil   Get a life.

David   Yeah. Get a life.

Phil   Oh oh oh. I've done it. I've pissed myself.

David   Stop it. Stop that.

Phil   Please. Please. Help me.

David   Clean yourself up.

Phil   I don't know how. Please. Please. Don't want to be
like this. Damp and pissy. You gotta . . .

David   Come on then. Alright. Alright.

David *removes* **Phil**'s *trousers and mops him down.*

Phil   Has it gone now? Did you make it go away?

David   Yes. All gone now.

Phil   You're clever. I like you. See I need you.
What do you do with this? (*The cloth.*)

David   You wash it.

Phil   How do you do that then?

Beat.

Phil   Do you want me to finish you off?

David   . . . Yes.

Phil   Yes *please.*

David   Yes please.

Phil   Twenty quid.

David   I'm sorry?

Phil   Twenty quid. Come on. Nothing's for nothing.
Twenty quid.

Scene Four

Flat.

Suzanne *videos* **Lorraine**, *who is eating.*

Suzanne   So what's that Lorraine?

Lorraine   It's a pizza.

Suzanne   What type of . . . ?

Lorraine   Cheese and tomato pizza.

Suzanne   A cheese and tomato pizza.

Lorraine   Want some?

Suzanne   No thank you.

Lorraine   If you want a bit . . .

Suzanne   No thank you.

Lorraine   Is that 'getting involved'?

Suzanne   . . . That's right.

Lorraine   You're not allowed to do that are you?

Suzanne   There doesn't seem to be . . . I can't see very much cheese.

Lorraine   You oughtta eat something.

Suzanne   In fact, I can't see any cheese at all.

Lorraine   That's right.

Suzanne   So . . . a cheese and tomato pizza with no cheese. That's a bit unusual.

Lorraine   There was cheese.

Suzanne   Yes?

Lorraine   But I scraped it off.

Suzanne   I see. / Scraped it off.

Lorraine   Yeah. Scraped it off. Go on. Taste it. It's nice.

Suzanne   Why did you scrape it off Lorraine? Don't you / like the cheese?

Lorraine   You'll waste away you will.

Suzanne   Why did you buy a cheese and tomato pizza and scrape off the cheese?

Lorraine   Do you think I'm weird?

Suzanne   I'm not here to pass judgement.

Lorraine   You think I'm weird.

Suzanne   No, no, no.

Lorraine   You think it's stupid, scrape off the cheese.

Suzanne   No.

Lorraine   Taste it.

Suzanne   ... No.

Lorraine   Maybe it is stupid.

Suzanne   Hey, we're all a bit stupid sometimes.
Sometimes I'm very stupid. Sometimes I'm totally bonkers.

Lorraine   You're not.

Suzanne   I am.

Lorraine   You're not.

Suzanne   So why did you scrape off the cheese Lorraine?

Lorraine   My mum used to scrape off the cheese.

Suzanne   I see. Your mum used to scrape off the cheese.

Lorraine   That's right.
Little bit. You know you want it.

Suzanne   Well ... thank you.

Lorraine   You're involved now.

Suzanne   Not really.

Lorraine   Put it down (*The camcorder.*) for a minute.

Suzanne   No.

Lorraine   You're always on the job you aren't you?

Suzanne   Not always, no. Just now ... I'm ... I'm on
the job now.
So. Your mum used to scrape off the cheese but now she
... She used to but now she ... Lorraine?

Pause.

Suzanne   Lorraine?

Lorraine   She died. Last month, she died.

Suzanne   I'm sorry.

Lorraine   Yeah, well done now, isn't it?

Long pause.

Suzanne   Lorraine . . . I'm sorry.

Long pause.

Lorraine   There's lots more in the freezer. You can have a whole one.

Suzanne   No. Thank you.

Lorraine   Alright then.

Suzanne *comes over. Hesitates. Hugs* **Lorraine**.

Lorraine   What was that for?

Suzanne   Just because . . . I didn't mean . . .

Lorraine   It's alright . . .

Suzanne   Yes?

Lorraine   Yeah. It was nice.

Pause. **Suzanne** *hugs* **Lorraine**. *Kisses the top of her head.*
Lorraine *laughs, kisses the top of* **Suzanne**'s *head. Pause.*
Suzanne *kisses* **Lorraine**'s *lips lightly.* **Lorraine** *laughs,*
kisses **Suzanne**'s *lips. Pause.* **Suzanne** *kisses* **Lorraine** *on the*
mouth for some time.

Lorraine   I didn't mean tongues.

Suzanne   No?

Lorraine   No. I didn't mean that.

Suzanne   Oh.

Suzanne *continues videoing.*

Lorraine   . . . It's not like I ever liked her. Used to lie awake sometimes. Used to lie awake and think: Wish you'd die. Wish you were dead you old witch. But now . . . now . . . I . . . I go down the shops the same time as her. I watch her programmes. I wear her clothes. I put on her clothes and I watch her programmes and I eat pizza like she used to eat pizza.

Suzanne I see.

Suzanne *puts down the camera.*

Lorraine You don't have to stop.

Suzanne I think maybe . . .

Lorraine I don't want you to stop.
And if the phone goes and it's the double glazing and that
I don't say: 'No. She's dead'. I say 'speaking'. I do her
voice and I say 'speaking'.

Suzanne Listen . . .

Lorraine I feel so empty.

Suzanne Listen, Lorraine let's . . .

Lorraine Why do I feel . . . ? It's not like I ever liked
her.

Suzanne *puts down the camera.*

Lorraine I told you not to stop.

Suzanne Lorraine, I'm just going to . . . hold you.
Nothing . . . Okay?

Suzanne *holds* **Lorraine**.

Suzanne That's it.

Suzanne*'s pager goes off. She ignores it. It carries on. She gets up,
reads the message.*

Suzanne I'm sorry. I've got to go.

Lorraine Alright then.

Suzanne I'm sorry. It's just . . .

Lorraine It's alright.

Suzanne Sorry. I know it's shitty. It's just very important.

Lorraine That's alright.

Suzanne No really. My . . . my baby's going to be born. Our . . . my partner . . .

Lorraine Your girlfriend?

Suzanne Yes. My girlfriend is having a baby. And . . . I've got to be there. I want to be there.

Lorraine Course.

Suzanne You going to be alright?

Lorraine Course.

Suzanne I'm sorry.

Exit **Suzanne**.

Lorraine (*calls*) You left your . . .

Front door slams.

Lorraine Jumper.

Scene Five

Drawing room.

Cardew (*off*) Colonel Moncrieff. Colonel Moncrieff.

Enter **Moncrieff** *followed by* **Cardew**.

Cardew It really is most urgent. One of my boys has been mislaid.

Moncrieff Mislaid, Mr Cardew? How careless.

Cardew Not through want of care. No. I am the most caring and watchful / of . . .

Moncrieff Just so.

Cardew My boys could not receive more attention. I am at / all times . . .

Moncrieff Of course. At all times.

Cardew But despite my care and attention and

instruction and . . . forgive me. It has been a great upset. This morning the fencing master called as usual. Instruction was about to begin when I noticed that one of the boys was missing. I called names, I counted heads. And Eustace . . . Eustace was nowhere to be found.

Moncrieff   Eustace?

Cardew   Mr Wilton.

Moncrieff   Ah, Mr Wilton.

Cardew   The search was begun immediately. Hither and thither, high and low. Willises, Drury Lane, the Savoy. But nothing. I am beside myself.

Enter **Constance***, heavily pregnant.*

Constance   Mr Cardew.

Moncrieff   No, my love. This is not proper.

Constance   I thought I heard voices.

Moncrieff   You must stay in your room.

Constance   Confinement is unbearable. I am so lonely.

Moncrieff   It is your burden.

Constance   Please. For a short while.

Cardew (*to* **Constance**)   Have you seen Mr Wilton? Didn't he visit here several times? Didn't he help you organise a little amateur theatricals?

Constance   With great enthusiasm. I fancy he may become a great actor.

Cardew   Eustace has a great many talents.

Moncrieff   I did not consider Mr Wilton a very suitable companion for my wife. Did I my love?

Constance   No. You did not.

Moncrieff   I found him to be a little too . . . effeminate.

Constance   He has grace.

Cardew He has a little too much grace about him, despite my efforts.

Moncrieff In fact, I find a great many of your boys a little too effeminate.

Constance My love.

Cardew I give my boys all the really manly virtues. To throw a discus, a javelin. To wrestle.

Constance *clutches her stomach.*

Cardew . . . I wonder . . . have you seen . . . ?

Moncrieff No. We have not seen Mr Wilton for several months.

Cardew Oh. Poor Eustace. The world will confuse him. He will be troubled. He'll be wanting me.

Constance It has started. Oh god. It has started.

Moncrieff Come. To your room.

Cardew If you should see Mr Wilton . . .

Moncrieff *and* **Constance** *exit.*

Enter **Augusta**.

Augusta Oh brother. At last.
But why don't you speak . . . ? How can you be so strange?

Cardew I think there must be some mistake.

Augusta Please forgive a young girl's ardent expression of emotion. I come from a nation of bog dwellers and my manners want polish.

Cardew I don't understand you.

Augusta This cursed brogue. I must struggle to sound English if I am to be understood. Brother, it is I. Augusta.

Cardew Augusta?

Augusta Am I to be treated as the poor relation? I know I have a want of means. But surely a want of means is not a hindrance in society? Want of character is the only serious hindrance and I have a very great deal of character.

Cardew I don't know you.

Augusta This is a blow. Not know me, Colonel Moncrieff?

Cardew There seems to be a misunderstanding.

Enter **Moncrieff**.

Cardew This is Colonel Moncrieff.

Augusta Brother. It is I – Augusta.

Moncrieff Welcome, welcome. You must forgive Mr Cardew. Such proximity to a member of the female sex is altogether strange to him.

Augusta You should marry Mr Cardew.

Cardew Marry? How should I find time for marriage when I have my hands so very full.

Moncrieff Indeed. We follow Mr Cardew's activities closely.

Cardew Yes. I am happy to say that the activities of the Belgrave Square Society for the Discovery and Betterment of Foundling Boys from the Lower Orders are reported in all the most philanthropic journals.

Moncrieff I was not referring to philanthropic journals.

Cardew No? What then?

Moncrieff Talk mainly. People talk a great deal about your activities.

Constance *(off) cries out.*

Cardew Good lord. What a terrible noise.

Moncrieff Not at all. It is the sound of labour.

Cardew Labour? Isn't that something that happens in Manchester?

Augusta   My poor sister.

Cardew   The fecundity of our species is a constant surprise to me.

Moncrieff   For a man such as yourself it must be.

Off, **Constance** *cries out.*

Cardew   Good Lord. How do you stand it?

Moncrieff   A soldier can bear almost anything. A great many of your boys run off don't they? What can you be doing to them?

Cardew   I don't know what you mean sir.

Moncrieff   Oh but I think you do sir.

Cardew   I give my boys the father they never had.

Moncrieff   And maybe the father they never wanted.

Cardew   I must find Eustace.

Moncrieff   He will return. To a father, surely he will return.

Cardew   Please, I can't bear to mislay another.

Moncrieff   Disgusting spectacle.

Cardew   Disgusting? How so? Disgusting?

Enter **Prism**.

Moncrieff   Ah this must be the new nanny.

Prism   Good evening, Colonel Moncrieff. Prism.

Cardew   Not disgusting.

Moncrieff   Thank goodness the modern age has realised the importance of dividing up our lives. Former ages, I believe, quite muddled up the aspects. Now we men can play billiards in the billiards room, smoke in the smoking room and relax in the library. And the ladies . . . well the ladies have their own worlds too.

Augusta Indeed. I hope you will allow me to sing one evening.

Moncrieff And then there is the world of childhood. Which is your burden.

Prism Yes sir.

Cardew I cannot allow 'disgusting'.

Moncrieff Today a child will be born and it will be taken instantly into your care.

Prism I'm ready sir.

Moncrieff As yet my wife is unaware of your arrival. In fact, as yet she is unaware that you exist at all. She has resisted all suggestion of wet nurses and nannies. She thinks she can be everything to the child. But if in time your care is excellent, I am sure she will come to like you a great deal.

Prism I hope so sir.

Constance *cries out.*

Moncrieff Anticipation. It is a dreadful thing.

Cardew I cannot allow my good name –

Moncrieff I shall be in the billiard room.

Exit **Moncrieff.**

Cardew 'Disgusting'. That is so unjust. When all I offer is care.

Augusta But still. A man cannot care for so many boys alone.

Cardew My boys will testify that I am always most kind. Kind and charitable.

Augusta You should find a companion Mr Cardew. One who can share your calling. A helpmate, a soulmate.

Cardew Maybe, in time . . .

Augusta   Search and you shall find.

Cardew   I must find –

Augusta   You must find a wife. A young woman. In her full bloom.

Cardew   No. No woman can understand my mission. No woman can care for my boys.

Augusta   Are you in *Burke's*?

Augusta *produces a copy of* Burke's Peerage.

Augusta   This dear volume has been my constant companion for the last three years. Sitting amongst those ignorant Oirish, waiting, waiting for . . . London . . . society . . . a new name.

Cardew   Please, / let me go.

Augusta   You have a town house, I know. But a country house? How many bedrooms? Are both your parents still living? / Do you smoke?

Cardew   No. No. No. I am not at all interested in marriage.

Augusta   Oh. Then maybe my dear brother is right. Maybe there is something a little . . .

Cardew   These insinuations are intolerable.

Augusta   Then marry and prove them wrong.

Cardew   I shall find Mr Wilton. I shall find him and bring him here and he will tell you, he will tell all of you, what an excellent guardian I am. You shall hear it from his mouth.

Exit **Cardew**.

Prism   Oh dear. It seems it is rather more difficult to lose a name than you thought.

Augusta   Take care. Nanny.

Prism   This must be your last season with any hope of

finding a husband, is it not?

Augusta   What would you know of marriage?

Prism   I am not very much interested in marriage. At least not while there are novels to be written.

Constance *cries out.*

Augusta   She calls. My poor sister calls.

Exit **Augusta**. **Prism** *sits. Opens her bag. Gets out her manuscript. Cradles it like a baby.*

Prism   Yes. Yes. Ssssh. Ssssh.

Scene Six

Under a bridge.

Phil *is fucking* **David**. **Phil** *pulls away.*

David   No. Don't stop. Don't stop.

Phil   Fifty quid.

David   I don't think I . . . I think you've had . . . Luncheon vouchers? AMEX?

Phil   Gotta be cash.

David *finds some money.*

David   It's all I've got left.

Phil   . . . Alright then.

Phil *carries on fucking* **David**. **David**'*s mobile rings.*

Phil   You gonna get that?

They continue fucking.

Phil   I think you better get it.

David *answers the mobile.*

David   Hello? Oh. Hi. I'm sorry. I'm sorry. What more

can I – ? I'm sorry. Well, I'm trying to get awa – yes, at
work. Look. I'm sorry. What more can I – ? Fuck you. I'm
sorry that I'm busy okay? I'm sorry I have to work. I'm
sorry that life is so fucking complicated. I love you. I love
you – Fuck.
(*To* **Phil**.) Don't stop. Don't stop.
Oh fuck it. Fuck it.

Phil *continues fucking* **David**.

David   My kid's been born.

More fucking.

Phil   Yeah?

More fucking.

Phil   Boy or a girl?

David *stops. Pushes last-number redial.*

David   Hi. Me. Boy or a girl? Well of course I care.
Because . . . because. I care alright? Boy or a girl? You . . .
child. Boy or a girl?
He wouldn't say.

Phil *goes to fuck him again.*

David   No.

Phil   You gotta let me finish.

David   I have to go. I should be there.

Phil   So. Wham. Bam. Thank you Dad.

David   I'm sorry.

Phil   Go on then. Piss off. Piss off. You leave me here.

David   Haven't you got a home to go to?

Phil   No.

David   Oh.

Phil   They don't let me in the hostel. I'm a handful.
You look after that kid, alright?

David Of course.

Phil They're gonna want someone looking over them. That's what we all want. And do you know who they're gonna want looking over them? They're gonna want you. You gotta be there for them.

David Here. My card. Call me.

Phil Might do.

David Well ... Whatever.

Phil I touch their bumps, you know, women expecting.

David Everyone does.

Phil But really I want to punch them. You ever want that?

David No.

Phil Kiss goodbye?

Scene Seven

Maternity ward. **Suzanne** *sits. Enter* **Tom**.

Tom He's on his way. That's what he said. On his way.

Suzanne Then I'm sure.

Tom It just makes me so fucking angry. To miss the birth. I wanted us to share that, you know?

Suzanne I know.

Enter **Mauretta**, *holding baby*.

Tom What did they say? Is he alright?

Mauretta Yes. He's alright now.

Tom But did they check ...?

Mauretta Yes. The doctor's had a look and ...

Tom I don't think that his breathing sounds ...

Mauretta   It's a floppy larynx.

Tom   So what does that . . . ?

Mauretta   His larynx is slightly . . . there's a potential that his larynx may block his breathing.

Suzanne   Oh god.

Mauretta   Potentially. But it's okay. We can cope with it. They're going to train us how to deal with it.

Tom   Alright.

Suzanne *kisses* **Mauretta**.

Suzanne   Isn't she a genius?

Tom   Yeah.

Suzanne   My fucking genius.

Beat.

Mauretta   They wanted to take him away.

Tom   Yes?

Mauretta   Yes. Snatch him away. Stick a little plastic marker on his wrist and shove him in a plastic box.

Tom   Well, I suppose they know what they're up to.

Mauretta   It doesn't seem natural. When what you want to do is hold on to him.

Tom   Of course you do.

Mauretta   You don't want to let go.

Suzanne   You need to sleep.

Mauretta   Bit later.

Tom   Must be knackered.

Mauretta   Yeah. And of course they lose them all the time.

Tom   No.

Mauretta   Oh yeah. There's always someone wandering around looking for a baby to grab.

Tom   Don't think so.

Mauretta   Maternity ward. Like a magnet for all those weirdos who want someone else's baby.

Suzanne   We'll stand guard, eh?

Mauretta   Yeah.
I had this woman on my show. Some girl took her baby. And the hospital had it all on video. The security camera. 'Could it be someone you know?' So they showed her the video, but you couldn't see the face because of course the camera was in the wrong fucking place. 'I can't see the face.' 'Oh, but there's a moment when she looks over her shoulder. Put it on freeze frame and you can catch the face.' But it's all blurry and you can never quite make it out. She watched it over and over but . . . They found the baby a week later in a dustbin.

Enter **David**, *wearing a plastic mask and carrying a bottle of champagne.*

David   'Over the hills and far away . . .'

Tom   Fucking hell.

David *takes off the mask.*

David   Present.

Suzanne   I don't think he's quite ready for that.

David   It's a boy?

Suzanne   Yeah. It's a boy. Jack.

David (*looks at baby*)   Who's a gorgeous boy then?

Tom   So, that makes it alright does it?

Suzanne   Let's get organised. We need to . . . he's got a breathing . . . a slight breathing problem. And we need to all be trained. So, let's organise . . .

Tom *and* **Suzanne** *get out diaries.* **David** *gets out an electronic organiser.*

Suzanne   How about tomorrow?

David   Tomorrow's bad for me.

Suzanne   Yes?

David   Yeah. Manchester tomorrow.

Tom   You didn't tell me that.

David   Course I did.

Tom   Do you get this?

Mauretta   Sometimes.

Tom   I get this all the time.

Mauretta   We book each other in. Works most of the time.

David   It's all a bit manic at the moment.

Tom   Meaning?

David   Meaning I've got no windows.

Tom   It's important. It . . . we all have to bond with him right from the beginning.

David   Bond. Right.

Tom   Otherwise he'll feel closer to . . .

Suzanne   Mummy and Mummy.

Daddy   Mummy and Mummy?

Tom   Exactly. Mummy and Mummy than he does to . . .

David   Daddy and Daddy?

Tom   Daddy and Daddy.

David   Listen, I'm not sure about Daddy and Daddy.

Tom   No? What then?

David Well, you as Daddy obviously –

Tom And you're . . . ?

David Uncle.

Tom Uncle?

David Uncle David. Sounds alright.

Tom Uncle David who's around when it suits him.

David No.

Tom Uncle David who pops into the nursery for ten minutes when he gets back from the gym.

David Look it was your sperm.

Tom Fuck you. Fuck you.

Exit **Tom**.

David Fuck. What am I supposed to . . . ?

Mauretta He's upset. He wanted you to be there for the birth.

David I was working.

Suzanne Yeah?

David Yeah.

Mauretta (*to* **Suzanne**) Managed to drag you away didn't we?

Suzanne I didn't need dragging. This girl. She's so . . . needy.

David Must be pleased to have you around.

Suzanne Maybe. Yes.

Enter **Tom**.

Suzanne (*to* **Mauretta**) Come on. Let's get you both to bed.

Exit **Suzanne** *and* **Mauretta**.

Tom   You should have said a long time ago if you don't want this.

David   I want it okay?

Tom   Sure?

David   Sure. I just – sometimes I feel like a bit of a tit being called Daddy.

Tom   Get used to it.

David   Yeah. I'm happy being a tit. Alright?

David *holds up the bottle of champagne.*

David   Drink?

Scene Eight

Office.

Lorraine *is waiting. Enter* **Suzanne**.

Lorraine   Hello.

Suzanne   Lorraine. This is a surprise.

Lorraine   Yeah. Hello.

Suzanne   . . . I'm in the middle of a presentation.

Lorraine   You left your jumper.

Suzanne   Did I?

Lorraine   Yeah. Left your jumper at mine.
It's a nice jumper. I haven't been wearing it much.

Suzanne   I have to get back. Look . . . you keep the jumper.

Lorraine   I can't do that.

Suzanne   Course you can.

Lorraine   No.

Suzanne   I want you to have it.

Lorraine   Alright. Thanks.

Suzanne   And now I have to . . .

Lorraine   I want to speak to you.

Suzanne   I'm busy.

Lorraine   I need to speak to you.

Suzanne   How about a taxi? Shall we send you back in a taxi? That would be a treat.

Lorraine   Don't talk to me like I'm a kid.

Suzanne   I'm not. I'm just . . .

Lorraine   Yeah. Yeah. Don't you fucking talk to me like I'm a . . . don't you patronise me.

Suzanne   I'm not. I've just got to –

Enter **David**.

David   I'm sorry.

Suzanne   Lorraine this is David.

Lorraine   Hello.

David   Well of course. I recognised you.

Lorraine   Yeah?

David   From your appearances on the television. With the pizza.

Lorraine *bursts into tears.*

Suzanne   Lorraine . . .

Suzanne *is unsure what to do. After a while,* **David** *puts an arm around* **Lorraine**.

David   Come on Lorraine.

Lorraine   She grassed me up.

David   What? Who grassed you up Lorraine?

Lorraine   She did. She did. Suzanne . . .

Suzanne   What? What?

Lorraine   She grassed me up.

Suzanne   Oh come on . . .

David   What do you mean Lorraine?

Lorraine   Told the council that I shouldn't be living there.

Suzanne   No.

Lorraine   Don't fucking lie. She's lying.

Suzanne   Why would I lie Lorraine?

Lorraine   You answered the phone. You spoke to them. 'Maggie? No one here called Maggie.' Don't say you didn't.

Suzanne   Well maybe I . . .

Lorraine   Yeah, yeah. And now I've lost it. I've lost my flat.

David   Oh dear.

Lorraine   Because that's not what you do. They call and they say 'Maggie' and I go 'speaking' and it's alright. But she . . . she . . . I've lost my flat.

Suzanne   Oh I'm sorry Lorraine. I'm sorry.

Lorraine   Fuck all use sorry is when you've got no home.

Suzanne   But I didn't know . . .

Lorraine   No – had to go and answer the phone.

Suzanne   I didn't know you were . . . defrauding . . .

Lorraine   Fuck off . . . fuck off.

David   Hey. Hey.

Lorraine   She wanted me to have that flat. My mum wanted me to have that flat.

David   Of course.

Lorraine   Just she never put my name on the book. But I'm supposed to be there. You just go 'speaking' when they go 'Maggie'. Alright?

David   Sure.

Lorraine   So what's she gonna do about it?

Suzanne   I don't see what I can do about it.

Lorraine   You must know people. With houses and that.

Suzanne   Well . . .

Lorraine   I can get benefit.

Suzanne   No. No. I wish I could help, I wish there was a way to . . . I really . . . but . . . please, you have to go now. I have to . . .

Lorraine   You owe me. You fucking owe me.

Suzanne   I don't think so.

Lorraine   Yeah. I let you in. I told you about myself. You were nice.

David   Come on Lorraine . . .

Lorraine   What am I gonna do? Got no mum. Got no home. What am I gonna do?

Pause.

David   You've got a spare room.

Suzanne   No.

David   Maybe for a few days . . .

Suzanne   It's not a spare room. / It's a boxroom.

David   Just for a few days until Lorraine sorts herself out.

Suzanne   There's no window.

David   Still. For a day or so.

Suzanne   It's not a good time.

Lorraine   I don't mind.

Suzanne   With the baby just . . . it's impossible to sleep.

Lorraine   I don't mind.

Suzanne   No.

Lorraine   No mum. No home.

Lorraine *bangs her head very hard several times.*

Suzanne   Stop. Stop that. Stop her.

David *and* **Suzanne** *pull her away. A scuffle.* **Lorraine** *cries.*
Suzanne *holds her.*

Suzanne   Oh Lorraine. I'm sorry.

Lorraine   You gonna kiss me?

Suzanne   Look . . . a couple of days, alright?

Lorraine   Yeah?

Suzanne   And that's it.

Lorraine   Thank you. I'll get my stuff.

Suzanne   Lorraine, this doesn't mean . . . I don't want
you to rely on me okay?

Lorraine   Course.

Exit **Lorraine**.

David   Wooh. Kooky bitch.

Suzanne   Don't call her that.

David   Miss Kookyfuckingkookybitch. I reckon she's
taken a bit of a shine to you.

Suzanne   Oh come on.

David   That's what I reckon. And I reckon you've taken
a bit of a shine to Miss Kooky Bitch.

Suzanne   Lorraine.

David Miss Kooky / bitch Lorraine.

Suzanne Sexist cunt.

David Oh yeah?

Suzanne Yeah. You are a total sexist / fucking cunt.

David Love juice Lorraine, / I bet.

Suzanne Fuck off.

David Oooooh, Lorraine. Pizza? Just wait 'til I scrape off the cheese. / Munchmunchmunch.

Suzanne Listen. I'm not the one who missed the birth, who was . . .

David Yeah? What? Yeah?

Suzanne All I'm saying is there may be a bit of projection going on here. That's all I'm saying.

David Bollocks.

Suzanne Because Mauretta and me. Solid as a fucking rock. That's what I'm saying.

David And we're . . .

Suzanne Maybe you're projecting on to me and / Lorraine because . . .

David Listen me and Tom. Tom / and me . . .

Suzanne Bit of a glass houses scenario going on / I reckon.

David Bollocks.

Suzanne Oh yes? / Oh yes?

David Yes actually talking total / bollocks out of your arse that's what you're doing. Just because I catch a glimpse . . . just because I have a bit of a laugh about you and the kooky bitch you don't have to have a go at me right? You don't have to get the hump and start crapping on about stuff you know fuck all about. You know what

your problem is do you? Do you? I'll tell you. You've got
no sense of humour, zero. Zero. Zero. Nothing. And then
you start suggesting crap.

Suzanne I don't think so, I don't think so. It's not me
with the wandering dick. I mean, it's not hard to ... it's
blatant. And then you expect us to just pretend like we
havent noticed anything. Well, we notice, alright? We
notice. We know what you're like. Somebody should tell
Tom. How can Tom not notice what you're like? That's
what gets me. Does Tom know he lives with a dog with an
itchy dick? Does he? Does he? Does he?

Pause.

Why don't you have her? Why don't you and Tom ... ?

David Because we're ... me and Tom are ... we've
decided for a trial ... we're going to live apart for a while.

Suzanne Oh. I see.

David For a while.

Suzanne Alright.

Exit **Suzanne**. *Beat. Enter* **Lorraine** *with bags.* **David** *pushes
past her to exit. Pause. Enter* **Phil**.

Lorraine Hello.

Phil Do you work here?

Lorraine Yeah.

Phil Right.

Lorraine On and off.

Phil I'm looking for David.

Lorraine He's in a presentation at the moment.

Phil Right.

Lorraine But I can take a message.

Phil Tell him Phil's looking for him.

Lorraine I'll just find . . .

Lorraine *looks for pen and paper.*

Phil I've seen you before.

Lorraine Yeah?

Phil Yeah. On the video. With the tea bags.

Lorraine Oh yeah.

Phil These your bags?

Lorraine Yeah.

Phil Got no home?

Lorraine Oh yeah, but I'm going to stay with Suzanne. They want me to look after their kid.

Phil Like a nanny?

Lorraine Yeah. Like a nanny.

Phil Thought you worked here.

Lorraine Yeah. Well, I work here . . . and I'm a nanny.

Phil You'd be good with kids. You've got kind eyes.

Lorraine Yeah?

Phil Kind eyes, kind hands. Some people are just right for taking care of people.

Lorraine Yeah.

Phil You tell David I'm looking for him alright?

Lorraine Alright.

Phil I'll be seeing more of you.

Scene Nine

Bedsit.

Mobile rings. Enter **David**. *Answers mobile.*

David   Hello? Oh hi. What time is . . . ? Right. Oh right. Alright. Where have you been? Right. See you in a few minutes.

Exit **David**. *Mobile rings again. Enter* **David** *putting on trousers. Answers mobile.*

David   Hi. Oh. Hello. Yeah? Well, it's . . . It's a bit late. Can't we . . . ? Well, of course not. No. Why should I have someone here? Where are you . . . ? Yeah?

David *goes to window, waves.*

David   Yeah. Alright then. See you in a minute.

David *puts down the mobile.*

David   Fuck.

Exit **David**. *Pause. Doorbell rings. Enter* **David** *crosses, comes back in with* **Tom**.

Tom   I thought you might have found somewhere nicer.

David   It's alright.

Tom   More of a bedsit really.

David   It's a studio apartment.

Tom   Same thing.

David   As a temporary measure.

Tom   Yeah . . . temporary measure.
Listen I've been thinking and well . . . well, actually I've been missing you.

David   Yeah?

Tom   Yeah. Well actually I've been pretty fucking lost actually.

David   Can't live with me . . . ?

Tom   Can't live without you. Fucker eh?

David   Yeah.

Tom So, I just wanted to say . . . with the baby and everything. I think . . . you know, all the plans we had with the baby . . . and it's going to be difficult, I know that. I mean, I know I'm difficult and you're . . . well you're absolutely fucking impossible. But if that's the way it is then . . . yeah?

David . . . Yeah.

Tom Because whatever the hassle this has gotta be better than being on your own. Being on your own's miserable. And I don't want the kid growing up and you not being around, okay? That doesn't seem right.

Doorbell rings.

Tom Who's that?

David I dunno.

Tom Bit late to . . .

David Nutters. Yeah, nutters or junkies from the park. Or prostitutes. Pissed prostitutes.

Tom Yeah?

David Yeah. Happens all the time. Ignore them, they go away.

Doorbell rings.

Tom Maybe we should call the police.

David No.

Tom They shouldn't be doing that, middle of the night.

David Ssssh. Pretend no one's in.

Tom What?

David Sssshhh.

Doorbell rings again. Pause.

Phil (*off*) Hello. Hello.

Long pause.

Phil (*off*)   Hello. Hello. David.

Tom   He said 'David'.

David   Yeah?

Tom   Yes. He knows you.

David   No, no.

Phil (*off*)   Fucking hell. David. Come on.

Tom   Look –

David   No.

Tom   I'm going to sort this out.

Exit **Tom**.

David   Shit.

Phil (*off*)   Oh. Hello.

Tom (*off*)   Hello.

Phil   I'm looking for David.

Tom   You know David?

Phil   Yeah. Biblically.

Tom   Really? Then you'd better go through.

Enter **Phil** *followed by* **Tom**.

Phil   Hello.

David   Hello.

Phil   I need a bath.

David   Yeah?

Phil   I smell like shit in summer.

Tom   Oh, I think David quite likes that.

Phil   Yeah?

Tom   Oh yes, the oikier the better isn't that right?

David Listen.

Tom Oh yes. I should just let him fuck you as you are.

Phil No.

Tom No?

Phil He likes me to fuck him.

David Oh come on.

Tom Really? He always said it hurt when I tried to do it.

David Please.

Tom Couldn't take it could you my love? Still, I suppose when they're pre-pubescent . . .

Phil What you saying?

Tom Nothing.

Phil You saying my dick's small?

Tom Oh, come back to me when your balls have dropped.

Phil Fuck off. Fuck off.

Phil *starts to take off his clothes.*

David Look please . . .

Tom (*to* **David**) Come on then. You too – trousers off. Come on. Don't mind me. Trousers down and off you go. This I have got to see. Stick his smeggy little rancid cock up you. Come on. Come on.

David No.

Tom Because if that's what you want. If this little piece of human garbage is all you can aspire to then fine.

Phil Fuck off. / Don't you . . . Fuck off.

David Please. Please. Stop.

Phil You gonna let him talk to me like that?

David   Well I . . .

Phil   Don't you talk to me like that.

Tom   Oh don't worry. Don't you worry. I'm not going to talk to you – to you or to him – ever again.

David   Please . . .

Pause.

Phil   I'm gonna run my bath.

Exit **Phil**. *Pause.*

David   I'm sorry. I . . .

Tom   You know what? This is sad. It's just sad. It's just such a fucking tragedy when you're a grown-up and you're trying to live like you're nineteen. When all you can do is work so you can go to the gym and gossip and no pecs, no sex and live your shallow, shallow little life.

David   Yes? So what? So what do you want?

Tom   I want some kind of commitment.

David   So – up with the Wendy House. Up with the Wendy House and how did Mummy and Daddy do it and their mummy and daddy do it and let's be like them. Yeah and let's move to suburbia and / bleach those nets and twitch, twitch, twitch.

Tom   Oh fuck off, fuck off.

Exit **Tom**. *Pause. Enter* **Phil**, *a towel wrapped around him.*

Phil   Bath's running. Wanna share it?

David   No.

Phil   You can scrub all the tricky bits.

David   No. I can't handle . . . no.
I found your gear. In the cistern, I found your gear.

Phil   So?

David   So. I thought you were clean.

Phil I am.

David But you're still keeping your gear in my toilet?

Phil For emergencies.

David Yeah?

Phil For if I have an emergency. If I can't handle stuff.

David What stuff? You haven't got any stuff to handle.

Phil That's what you think.

David You've got it easy. You're safe. I feed you. I give you clothes. If you want me to wipe your bottom . . .

Phil I can't handle you. You do my head in.

David Oh come on.

Phil What you trying to make me into? What are you doing to me? Fucking poof's food. Fucking *queen's* clothes. That's not me. That's you that is. Well, maybe I don't want to be you . . .

David And what do you want to be?

Phil I dunno . . . me.

David And what are you exactly?

Phil I dunno.

David Junkie? Junkie cunt who doesn't see his own kid? Smelly little street boy druggie?

Phil Fuck off.

David I'm trying to make you into something.

Phil Yeah. Your bumchum. Well, I ain't gonna do it anymore. I ain't gonna stick it up you anymore. Alright? Where you going?

David I'm going to throw it away.

Phil *pushes* **David** *over, kicks him.*

Phil What? What you gonna do that for? Fuck you. Fuck you.

David I want you to . . . just leave me alone.

Phil I'm not doing that.

David I want you to go.

Phil No. Don't go after him. Stay with me. Stay. I'm not going. I'll be here when you come back.

Exit **David**.

Phil Shit. Shit.

Phil *exits to bathroom. Returns with his gear. Injects.*

Cardew (*off*) Eustace. Eustace. Eustace. Eustace.

Enter **Cardew**.

Phil Fuck.

Cardew Eustace. Oh Eustace. You were wrong to leave me.

Phil Yeah?

Cardew You were foolish.

Phil Yeah?

Cardew I shall forgive if you will solemnly undertake never to be mislaid again.

Phil Alright.

Cardew You solemnly swear?

Phil I solemnly swear. Forgive me?

Cardew You are forgiven.

Phil You gonna fuck me?

Cardew Eustace.

Phil I need a fuck.

Cardew It's not right to talk of such things.

Phil   You've gotta fuck me.

Cardew   We can be brothers. We can be comrades. We can fight alongside each other but . . .

Phil   I'm only asking for a fuck.

Cardew   Oh Eustace. Not the gutter. The stars.

Phil   Think you can do better?

A bath appears.

Cardew   Get in the tub Eustace.

Phil   What are you? Social worker?

Cardew   Eustace.

Phil   Don't call me that. I'm not Eustace.

Cardew   But . . . You have his face.

Phil   I'm not Eustace.

Cardew   Then I have been horribly deceived. Go. Go.

Phil   I'm not gonna go.

Cardew   Leave now.

Phil   Please. Let me stay. I'll be Eustace. I can be whatever you want me to be. How does he speak? Like this? Like this?

Cardew   He has a little too much of the aesthete about him.

Phil   Like this?

Cardew   You have him. I shall save you. You are ready to submit?

Phil   I've always wanted to be saved. But no one's offered before.

Cardew   What's your name?

Phil   Phil.

Cardew   Well, that can be changed.

Phil   Don't call me Eustace.

Cardew   Of course not. That would only lead to muddle.
Two Eustaces. I wouldn't do that. Eustace will return and
then think of the muddle.

Phil   So what you going to call me?

Cardew   I'll choose later, after some reflection.

Phil   So for now . . . I'm nothing. I've got no name.

Cardew   For the present.

Phil   I like that.
No clothes. No name.
(*He makes baby noises.*)

Cardew   Please. No.

Phil (*baby noises*)   Dadda. Dadda.

Cardew   This is undignified. Get in the tub.

Phil *gets in the tub.* **Cardew** *washes him.*

Cardew   We live in a sorry age. We have forgotten the
most precious teaching of the Ancients. A boy cannot reach
maturity in the family home. The family cloys. It crushes.
A boy knows this. He longs for the disciplines of the
Ancients. A boy waits for the moment. A man will arrive.
An older man. Elected by the community. One day he
appears at the family home. The mother and father
tremble. They knew that this day must come. But still it
has sent a deep fear into their hearts and they have not
dared to tell the boy that this moment will come. But now
it has come. The moment has arrived. The stranger is
here.
And he takes the boy's hand. 'Come. Come with me.'
The boy turns bewildered and looks to his parents. What is
happening? Tears roll down the parents' cheeks but they
nod as if to say: You must go. You must submit.
And the stranger takes the boy and they go into the hills.

A long journey until they find a goat. And they kill the
goat and they skin the goat and the boy is dressed in the
goat skin and he drinks the goat's blood.
And he sleeps in the hills with the stranger. And every day
– a new conquest. A bison, a horse, an elephant.
Weeks later the boy goes home. And his parents are
different and he realises that they will do anything he says.
He realises that he has power. He is a man.
There. You're done. Up.

Cardew *wraps the towel around* **Phil**.

Phil   Mmmmmm.

Phil *reaches for his clothes*.

Cardew   No. These are not suitable.

A set of Victorian clothes appear.

Cardew   These are for you.

Phil   My guardian. I always knew I had a guardian.
Didn't I always say I had a guardian? My unfortunate
guardian.

Scene Ten

Drawing room.

Phil *is in the Victorian clothes. He sings a Victorian ballad as*
Cardew *watches*.

Phil   I can't do this.

Cardew   Of course you can do it.

Phil   Alright. I don't want to do it.

Cardew   John. Don't be wilful.

Phil   I don't like John. Why do you call me John?

Cardew   Because it is both plain and becoming.

Phil   I don't want to be plain and becoming.

Cardew You will be whatever I decide you should be.

Phil Why can't I be called something else?

Cardew What? Jack?

Phil I don't know. Something else.

Cardew They will be through in a few minutes. After three. One two three.

Phil *sings.*

Cardew Well, it is not accurate but then anyone can sing accurately. But it is sung with great feeling, which is all that is required in polite society. The posture just a little more . . .

Cardew *arranges* **Phil**.

Phil Why can't I stand naturally?

Cardew Nature always benefits from a little rearrangement.

Phil I feel uncomfortable.

Cardew And a wilful nature must be watched at all times.
Now, I shall fetch them. We will be through shortly. The chin just a little higher.

Exit **Cardew**.

Phil Horrid postures. Horrid chins and horrid, horrid music.

Enter **Prism** *with pram and handbag. She has a bloody nose.*

Prism Excuse me. Excuse me. I . . .

She faints.

Phil Fuck.

Phil *holds* **Prism**.

Phil Come on. Come on.

Prism   Pray forgive me.

Phil   You alright?

Prism   Oh yes. Quite well thank you.

She stands, faints again. She recovers.

Prism   Oh dear.

Phil   What happened?

Prism   I have been the victim of an alarming incident.

Phil   Yeah?

Prism   Yes. I alighted, with some difficulty as I had the child in the perambulator, upon an omnibus in Gower Street which, as we turned into Bloomsbury Square, overturned, depositing me on the pavement.

Phil   Then you must be a Fallen Woman.

Prism   No. I assure you.

Phil   I've always wanted to meet a Fallen Woman.

Prism   Young man, I am quite unfallen.

The baby cries.

Phil   The child is calling for you.

Prism   Oh it is quite alright. No great damage done. Oh.

She opens the handbag.

Prism   Oh no. Oh no. Wretched temperance beverage. Cursed omnibus. Oh, what is to become of us?

Phil   What is it?

Prism   A temperance beverage, which I bought in Leamington in a moment of extravagance, has exploded in the upset and – oh, look at my manuscript. Just look at it. Maybe it can be saved. If I hurry. Please, will you wait with the baby for a while?

Phil   I can't do that.

Prism For a very short while, while I clean –

Phil No.

Prism He will be no bother.

Phil Don't leave me alone with it. Please. Please. Take it with you.

He pushes the pram to **Prism**.

Phil Take it with you.

She pushes the pram to **Phil**.

Prism Men are such cowards. For a moment.

He pushes the pram back.

Phil It won't be safe. You can't trust me.

Prism But I do. I do.

Phil I hurt people. I hurt myself. I done a bad thing. I shouldn't have did what I did to her. I know that now.

Prism Please. My manuscript is spoiling.

Phil Listen. Listen. Somebody's got to listen.
My kid. My kid. She's five. Then. She's five. We've got it all. Got a flat. Her mum's there. I'm there. And yeah, alright, we've both got a habit, but we're coping, okay? We're controlling it, it's not controlling us.
But I'm behind with my payments. And my dealer's giving me hassle. I mean, he's supplying but he's giving a lot of grief.
And I'm, 'You'll get your money. You'll get it.' Fuck knows how.
And one day he goes: 'Let me fuck the kid. Quick fuck with the kid. I'll be careful – it's not like I'm gonna split her or nothing. Ten minutes and I'll let you off.'
And I'm: 'No. You perv, you nonce. No.'
And it goes on. Months. 'Let me fuck the kid.' 'No.'
But then he stops supplying and you hold out, you're going fucking turkey but, you're a dad. Your instincts won't let you . . .

Until. Yeah. Until . . .

Prism   I don't understand you. What strange words you use.

Exit **Prism**.

Cardew (*off*)   Through here. We're all ready.

Enter **Cardew**, **Augusta**, **Moncrieff** *and* **Constance**. *They sit and wait, looking at* **Phil**.

Cardew   John?

Pause.

Cardew   John?

Pause.

Cardew   John.

Phil   I'm not John. You can't do this to me. You're fucking me up. You find someone else alright? You looked after me, you sorted me out. I'm grateful. But I'm moving on. You gotta find someone else.

Cardew   No. I don't want that.

Phil   You're a nice bloke. You'll find someone.

Cardew   I don't want that. I want you. I love you.

Phil   I don't want you to love me.

Cardew   I don't want to love you but . . .

Phil   I'm not like you. I can't be like you.

Cardew   Stay.

Exit **Phil**.

Cardew   John.

Moncrieff   Leave him be.

Cardew   But suppose he should escape.

Augusta   Escape?

Cardew   Please.

Exit **Cardew**. *The baby cries.*

Moncrieff   Why is the child left unattended?

Constance   I don't know.

Moncrieff   Where is the nanny? This won't do at all.
Prism! Prism!

Exit **Moncrieff**.

Augusta   Unreliable creature. I knew from the moment I
saw her on the platform she was not to be trusted.

Constance   How is our mother?

Augusta   Oh don't talk to me of her. I detest our mother.

Constance   Augusta, no.

Augusta   Our mother is of the sorry opinion that Ireland
is a woman in spirit and that the spirit of Ireland resides in
her.

Constance   Yes?

Augusta   A delusion which has led her to write many
mystic speeches and much inflammatory poetry.

Constance   But still, she is our mother.

Augusta   Really, this modern mania for acknowledging
one's parents after birth seems to me to be quite senseless.

Constance   You shouldn't say such things.

Augusta   Mothers should have their eyes plucked out.
Blindness is a very attractive thing in a woman.

Constance   How cold you are.

Augusta   Although you of course will be an excellent
mother.

Constance   Yes. This is of me. This came from me.

Constance *picks up the baby.*

Constance   Nothing. I feel nothing.

Scene Eleven

Corridor.

Phil (*off*)   Gobbledbybubblygobble. Hehhehhaa.
Go up. Go down. Go all the way up. Go all the way
down.
Uh oh. Uh oh. Uh oh.
Tastic. Tastic. Tastic. Hehehahahaaa.

Baby cries. Enter **Lorraine** *putting her clothes on. Enter* **Phil** *in
the plastic mask.*

Phil   Again. Again. Again. Again.

Lorraine   He wants me.

Phil   No bye-byes. No bye-byes.

Lorraine   I gotta go to him.

Phil   Tastic. Tastic. Again. Again.

Lorraine (*laughs*)   I told you no.

Phil   Tinky. Tinky-winky.

Lorraine   You're mad you.

Phil   Oh oh oh.

Lorraine   Bye bye Tinky-winky. Bye bye.

Phil   Again. Again.

Phil *grabs* **Lorraine**.

Lorraine   Off. Get off me.

Phil   Again. Again.

Lorraine   I told you. No.

Pause. **Phil** *takes off the mask. They kiss.*

Lorraine   Look. I got responsibilities.

Phil   Too right. This (*His erection.*) – this is your
responsibility.

Lorraine   No. That's well . . .

Phil   Yeah?

Lorraine   Well that's a laugh innit?

Phil   Oh, a laugh right. Yeah. Tubbyhaha.

Lorraine   Yeah. That's a giggle.

Phil   No. You're involved now.

Lorraine   Please. I've got a kid to look after. I don't
want to let them down. I was only supposed to be here for
a few days. But they asked me to stay on. 'Cos I'm good
with him.

Phil   What they need you for?

Lorraine   He's needy. They're busy. He's ill. They can't
cope.

Phil   They should learn to cope.

Lorraine   Come and have a look at him.

Phil   No.

Lorraine   Come on. He's gorgeous. You'll like him.

Phil   No.

Lorraine   He'll like you. I know he will.

Phil   I'm not good with kids. They don't like me.

Lorraine   You scared of him?

Phil   No . . . yes.

Lorraine   I love him. I never felt like I understood
anyone before. Before, everyone I met . . . I'm talking,
they're talking. But I never understood them. I always felt
like a kid. But him. I understand him, he understands me.
I like that.

Phil They're gonna use you, you know that? Use you to bring up the kid then soon as it can stand on its own two feet they're gonna push you out, you know that?

Lorraine No. They're not gonna do that.

Phil They will. You watch. I wouldn't do that. You come with me. I'm not gonna push you out.

Lorraine You're grown up now. You grow up and you're alone. You gotta do things by yourself.

Phil Can't do everything by yourself.

Lorraine No?

Phil No. Some things you gotta do together.

Phil *slips his hands inside* **Lorraine***'s knickers and starts to masturbate her.*

Phil Do you like that?

Lorraine Yeah.

Baby cries.

Phil He's calling for you.

Lorraine Yeah.

Phil He can wait for a minute. Alright?

Lorraine . . . Yeah. Where do you get those clothes?

Phil Off a poof.

Lorraine That's what I thought. You a poof?

Phil No. But I used a poof. Got to use who you can until you grow up, haven't you?

Lorraine Yeah.

Phil But I don't need them anymore. I'll get rid of them soon as I can.

Beat.

Lorraine I've got my mum's knickers on.

Phil Yeah?

Lorraine I'm wearing my mum's knickers.

Phil Does she know you've got them?

Lorraine She's dead.

Phil Nice.

Baby cries.

Lorraine I gotta go to him.

Phil In a minute.

Phil *puts the mask on* **Lorraine**, *continues to masturbate her.*

Phil I'm ready now. To be my own person. Always had something controlling me. The smack. And people. Didn't know who I was so I let people control me. But I'm past that now. I'm gonna find out who I am. Do you wanna find out who you are? Not a nanny. That's not you. You're . . .

Phil *moves to go down on* **Lorraine**.

Phil Yeah?

Lorraine Yeah.

Phil *goes down on her. After a while, she pulls away.*

Lorraine No. I gotta go to him.

Exit **Lorraine**.

Phil Tubbytastic.

Scene Twelve

Boxroom

Lorraine *is getting ready to go out. She is wearing a smart dress.* **Suzanne** *watches.*

Lorraine What do you think?

Suzanne   Oh yes. I like it.

Lorraine   It's alright isn't it?

Suzanne   It's great. Suits you.

Lorraine   You reckon?

Suzanne   Oh yes. You look great.

Lorraine   Like the one you've got.

Suzanne   I suppose it is – yes.

Lorraine   I saw you wearing it and I thought – That's nice.

Suzanne   Well, good . . .

Lorraine   I mean it's not yours. I bought it. But it's like yours.

Lorraine *applies lipstick.*

Lorraine   Hot blooded.

Suzanne   Yes?

Lorraine   That's what they call it. Is your one Hot Blooded?

Suzanne   No. I don't think so. No. Well . . . I'm sure that'll be appreciated. Hot Blooded.

Lorraine   Oh yeah. He'll like this.

Baby cries.

Lorraine   I'll go / to him.

Suzanne   No, no, no.

Lorraine   I think he wants me.

Suzanne   Mauretta's looking after him.

Cries die away.

Suzanne   There.

Mauretta (*on baby alarm*)   Yes. Yes. Mummy's here.

Lorraine   Can you. . . ?

Lorraine *turns.* **Suzanne** *does up her dress.*

Suzanne   So how's it going? With this boy?

Lorraine   I like him.

Suzanne   And he likes you?

Lorraine   I reckon.

Suzanne   So . . . what's he like?

Lorraine   Nice.

Suzanne   Well, that's a good start.

Lorraine   Yeah. Nice. And . . . rich.

Suzanne   Rich? Really?

Lorraine   Yeah. Really rich. With stocks. And shares and that.

Suzanne   Lucky you.

Lorraine   Oh yeah. In the City. Selling and buying. On a computer screen. Tokyo. New York and that.

Suzanne   Job like that must involve quite a bit of travelling.

Lorraine   Travel, of course, yeah, travel. He's going to be a millionaire by the time he's twenty-five. He won't want me to do this much longer.

Suzanne   Maybe, we should start looking for / another nanny.

Lorraine   No, no. You don't need to do that.

Suzanne   But if you're going to be / moving on . . .

Lorraine   No.

Suzanne   No?

Lorraine   I told him . . . I persuaded him to let me stay. 'Cos I'm too attached to you.

Suzanne Does he come here?

Lorraine Not really.

Suzanne Never?

Lorraine Well ...

Suzanne Sometimes?

Lorraine Of course sometimes ...

Suzanne Often?

Lorraine No, not often. He doesn't like it here. He's not comfortable. He's used to ... y'know ... bigger. Posher.

Suzanne I see.

Enter **Mauretta**.

Mauretta Fast asleep now.

Lorraine I'll look in on my way out.

Mauretta No need.

Lorraine Just have a / quick look.

Mauretta Best to leave him be.

Lorraine Alright then.

Mauretta Actually, Lorraine, we wanted a word with you.

Lorraine Yeah?

Mauretta Just a quick word. Won't take a few minutes.

Lorraine Alright.

Mauretta We just wanted to say ... we'd appreciate it if you didn't bring your boyfriend back here.

Lorraine Alright.

Mauretta And we'd particularly appreciate it if you didn't use our bed ...

Lorraine You / what?

Mauretta   For your sexual / activities.

Lorraine   I don't.

Mauretta   You don't?

Lorraine   No. Course I don't.

Mauretta   Because . . .

Lorraine   Because that would be wrong.

Mauretta   Yes. We're agreed. That would be wrong.

Suzanne   All we're trying to say is . . . this is a job. That's all we want to say. I know the pay's pretty shitty. But we pay what we can and we expect you to do your job.

Lorraine   I know, I know.

Suzanne   And we feel guilty.

Mauretta   Terribly guilty.

Suzanne   This room should be nicer . . .

Lorraine   I'm not complaining.

Suzanne   But that's the deal.

Lorraine   I know.

Mauretta   And we expect you to give him your undivided attention.

Lorraine   I do.

Mauretta   But you can't. If you're . . . entertaining then you can't be giving him your undivided attention.

Lorraine   I do give him my . . . I'm going now. He'll be waiting for me.

Mauretta   Wait . . . You're lying to us.

Lorraine   We're going to a restaurant. The table's booked.

Mauretta   Please. You're lying / to us.

Lorraine Don't you call me a liar. You got no right to call me that. I don't have to listen to this. I'm going now.

Mauretta We've been monitoring your activities.

Lorraine You what?

Mauretta We installed . . . there have been cameras watching you.

Lorraine (*laughs*)

Mauretta Yes. Really. There have been video / cameras . . .

Lorraine What do you fucking do that for?

Suzanne He's our child. He's fragile. He has to be looked after properly. We can't allow him to be neglected.

Mauretta We hoped that we were just being paranoid. That everything / was alright.

Lorraine What is this?

Suzanne You neglect him. He can cry. He can shout.

Lorraine That's not right.

Mauretta Do you want to watch it? Do you want me to show it to you?

Lorraine No.

Mauretta And I can see why this has happened. It's understandable. No girl wants to be tied to a baby for two pounds an hour when . . .

Lorraine It's not like that.

Mauretta But. We'd like you to leave.

Lorraine No.

Mauretta We'd appreciate it if you were to look for somewhere else.

Lorraine No. I'm not doing that. I'm not going. I like this job. (*To* **Suzanne.**) I bet you don't want me to go.

You don't want to lose me do you?

Suzanne I . . .

Lorraine Yeah, yeah. She wants me to stay.

Suzanne Lorraine . . . We both want you to go.

Beat.

Lorraine She kissed me.

Suzanne No.

Lorraine Yes she did. With her tongue. Lezzy kiss she did on me. Big lezzy kiss.

Baby cries again.

Lorraine He wants me.

Mauretta No.

Lorraine He's calling for me.

Mauretta I told you no.

Mauretta *pushes* **Lorraine** *back.*

Lorraine Fuck off. Fuck off you cow. I'll fucking have you you cow.

Lorraine *attacks* **Mauretta**. **Suzanne** *pulls her off.*

Mauretta I want you out of my house.

Lorraine You need me. He needs me. Someone's gotta be here for him. You can't do it. You're out. You work.

Mauretta That's right. We work.

Lorraine So you need . . .

Mauretta We work so that he can have a future. He's got to have an education. He's not going to end up like . . .

Lorraine What? What?

Mauretta He's not going to be a two-pound-an-hour person.

Lorraine   Fuck you. Fuck you.

Exit **Mauretta**.

Suzanne   I'm sorry it all got ... We're just trying ... we have to do what's best for our son.

Lorraine   He likes me.

Suzanne   Yes. He does.

Lorraine   More than he likes you.

Mauretta (*on baby alarm*)   There. There. Alright now. She's going.

Lorraine   And more than he likes her.

Scene Thirteen

Suzanne *is watching a video*.

Baby cries on video.

Phil (*on video*)   He's calling for you.

Lorraine (*on video*)   Yeah.

Phil (*on video*)   He can wait for a minute. Alright?

Enter **Mauretta**.

Mauretta   No. Don't love. Come on.

Suzanne   I want to watch it.

Mauretta   No. Come on.
Please. I don't want to watch it.

Suzanne   Then go somewhere else.

Mauretta   I'm not. You go somewhere else. I'm not having this. This doesn't make it better.

Suzanne   So – you gonna make it better? How you gonna do that? Come on then. Come on. You make it better.

Mauretta   Is it true . . . ?

Suzanne   What?

Mauretta   What she said, that you / kissed her.

Suzanne   No. Why should I . . . ? No.

Doorbell. Exit **Mauretta***, enters again with* **David***.*

David   Shit. Shit
So . . . some boy helped her take the baby?

Mauretta   That's right. Her boyfriend.

David   So. Who is this boy? Did you give a description?
You know what he looks like?

Suzanne   Oh yes.

Suzanne *rewinds the video.*

Phil (*on video*)   I'm ready now. To be my own person.
Always had something controlling me.

Suzanne   Can't see his face now but . . .

Phil (*on video*)   The smack. And people. Didn't know who I
was so I let people control me.

Suzanne   In a minute you can . . .

Phil (*on video*)   But I'm past that now. I'm gonna find out
who I am. Do you wanna find out who you are?

Suzanne   There. That's him.

Suzanne *pauses the video.*

David   I see.

Suzanne   Recognise him?

David   No.

Suzanne   Seen him before?

David   No. Don't think so. Why should I have seen him
before?

Suzanne Just your type.

David Oh yeah? Oh yeah? And what are we saying /
here? What's that supposed to mean?

Suzanne What are we saying? What are we saying?
We're saying that maybe / on one of your adventures . . .

David Fuck off. I don't need this. / Fuck you. Cunt.

Suzanne Yes, just maybe when you've been working
your way across London then maybe you might have come
across . . .

David Fuck off.

Suzanne I'm saying that maybe a father, / maybe a
dad –

Mauretta Hey come – she / doesn't – come on . . .

Suzanne Maybe somebody who wanted to be a dad /
could be putting it about a little bit less that's what I'm
saying.

David Instead of what? Videoing it all? Getting it all on
tape is that what we're saying? Coming home to watch
eight hours of video just so we can feel like Mummy? Is
that / what we're saying?

Suzanne I was watching out. I was watching out for
him.

David Oh, / well done. Well done you.

Mauretta Shut up. You're adults the pair of you. You
wanted to be Mummy. You said that.

Suzanne Yeah.

Mauretta And you wanted to be Uncle.

David Yeah.

Mauretta So fucking act like adults for fuck's sake.

Enter **Tom** *with food.*

Tom I thought we should eat. You need to eat something.

David Hello . . .

Tom Fuck. What's he . . . What's he doing here?

David Please . . .

Tom I don't want him here. I don't want you here.

David Listen. I fucked up alright? I fucked up big time. But now I know . . . I need you. Hold me.

Tom *holds* **David**. **David** *cries*. **Suzanne** *rewinds the video. Presses play. On video:*

Phil (*on video*) Didn't know who I was so I let people control me.

David Oh no. Please don't . . .

Phil (*on video*) But I'm past that now. I'm gonna find out who I am.

Suzanne (*to* **Tom**) This is him.

Long pause.

David He's a boy I . . . / I met a boy and he had no one and he needed to be looked after, alright? That's all it was. Looking after him. And I got attached. I shouldn't have done that. But what am I supposed to do? What am I fucking supposed to do? And I wanted to get rid of him. I should have got rid of the cunt but I was too weak. I was used. He was using me.

Tom Boy? Destroyed / everything now. For a boy. Some boy to fuck you and you destroyed everything. I can't do this anymore. Waiting for you, wanting you, forgiving you. I'm not doing that anymore. I've been so weak but now. I hate you. I feel hate for you. It could have been so good. The baby could have brought us together. But you couldn't handle – had to ruin everything.

Suzanne A boy, a boy. I knew it. I told you. Fucking

around. Always got your dick up somebody's arse. Always
using work, using me as your excuse because you've got the
urge, because you're looking for a shag. How many times
have I lied for you? How many times have I lied to Tom?
You did this. My baby's gone and you did this with your
itchy dick. Cunt. / Cunt. Cunt.

Mauretta   Shut up. Fucking SHUT UP.

Pause.

Mauretta   *My* baby. They took *my* baby.

Tom   Our baby.

Mauretta   My baby.

Tom   He loves me. He'll be missing me.

Mauretta   And what did you do? At the end of the day
what did you actually do?

Tom   I . . .

Mauretta   You wanked into a cup.

Tom   It makes me Dad. I'm a father.

Mauretta   It makes you nothing. You're like him. You're
like her. You're nothing. All of you. I had him. And I want
him back. And we're going to live together, him and me
and I'm going to watch him grow and I won't even tell
him that you exist. And maybe you'll interview him one
day, and maybe you'll teach him one day, and maybe
you'll try and sleep with him one day and you won't even
know who he is. He won't know you. Just me. That's all
he needs.

Tom   All of us.

Mauretta   All of us? All of us doesn't work. Look at you.

Mauretta *moves to go.*

Suzanne   Where are you . . . ?

Mauretta   No. I don't want you. You go to her. You go

to Lorraine. Go and kiss Lorraine.

Exit **Mauretta**.

David   I'm going to look for them. I . . .

Exit **David**.

Tom   I'm always looking after people. I hate that. Why do I always look after people? What I want now is someone looking after me.

Suzanne   Yes.

Tom   Hold me.

Suzanne   No.

Scene Fourteen

Phil *is bathing the baby.*

Phil   And so now there's three of them. The mum and the dad and the kid. And they've got a flat. Because that's important. And the mum and the dad have got a habit. But that's alright. Listen, it's alright. And there's a dealer. He's a bad man. And he wants to do really bad things to the kid. And the dad says: 'No. I'm not going to let you do that. I'm a father. No.' But the months go on and the dealer keeps coming back. 'Let me do bad things to the kid.' 'No.'
Then he stops supplying. But now he's a dad, he can fight it. He can go turkey this time and get through it.
And finally the dealer comes for the kid and the dad says: 'I'm free of you. I've got no habit and I'm free of you and I never want to see you again.' And the dealer starts to shake, and then he turns red like a furnace and then smoke comes out of his ears and he burns up until there's just a pair of shoes lying there and they're full of ash and that's the end.

Enter **Lorraine** *with food.*

Phil   There – you're done.

Phil *takes the baby out of the bath and wraps it in a towel.*

Lorraine   Cake or bread and butter?

Phil   Bit of both.

Phil *places the baby in a cardboard box crib at the end of the bed.*

Lorraine   You're good with him.

Phil   Yeah.

Lorraine   See. I knew you would be. You're a natural.

Phil   We're doing alright.

Lorraine   Yes, you are. He's a bit of natural isn't he Jack?

Phil   I was thinking. Jack. I don't like Jack. That's their name for him.

Lorraine   What then?

Phil   I don't know. Something else. A name we give him.

Lorraine   You got an idea?

Phil   Yeah. Yeah. I know. I know.

Phil *picks up the baby, goes to put him in a bag.*

Lorraine   What you doing?

Phil   Just for a moment.

Lorraine   He don't like it in there.

Phil   For a moment. How long did you have him in there?

Lorraine   That was different, that was. I had to do that. To get him out. Save him.

Phil   Only take a minute.

Phil *opens the bag.*

Phil   Bye-bye Jack. Bye-bye.

Phil *puts the baby in the bag.*

Phil   Come here.

Lorraine *goes over to* **Phil**. *They stand over the bag.*

Phil   No more past. Begin again. Begin now. Yeah?

Lorraine   Yeah.

Phil *reaches down and takes out the baby.*

Phil   Hello Eustace.

Lorraine   Eustace? You're mad you.

Phil   It's alright.

Lorraine   It's different.

Phil   Suits him.

Lorraine   Alright then. Eustace.

She takes the baby and puts it in the box.

Lorraine   Night, night. Eustace. Night, night.

Baby cries.

Lorraine   Oh. He's gone and wet himself again. Where the nappies?

Phil   None left.

Lorraine   I thought you got more.

Phil   I forgot.

Lorraine   He needs a clean one.

Phil   I'll go and get some.

Lorraine   No. You sit there and eat your tea. I'll get them.
Back soon. Alright?

Phil   Alright.

Exit **Lorraine**. *Baby cries louder.* **Phil** *walks it up and down.*

Phil   Oh no, come on. Oh no.

Enter **Cardew**.

Cardew   Oh help me. Please you must help me.

Phil   I don't want to see you.

Cardew   Hide me. I am in great danger. There has been the most terrible talk about the Belgrave Square Society. They say I do the most awful things to my boys. And now the barbarians . . . a crowd of the most barbaric kind has attacked us. My home is on fire and the boys . . . the boys have been taken away from me.

Phil   That's what you get, you nonce.

Cardew   John.

Phil   I'm not John.

Cardew   They. are here. Hide me.

Phil   No. See this? I've got a kid to look after.

Cardew   You owe me this much.

Phil   I don't owe you anything.

Cardew   I brought you naked and alone. What is his name? Who are his parents? Can he speak? Only his own language. He hasn't learnt our tongue. Somebody must teach him to speak. Somebody must name him. I will be that person. And so I gave you everything.

Phil   I took everything. So I could make myself into a person and now I'm a person, I don't need you anymore. Used you to get what I wanted and now I don't need you.

Cardew   No. You are nothing. Without me you are nothing.

Phil   I don't want you. Go. Go.

Enter **Augusta**.

Augusta   He is here. The invert is here.

She kicks **Cardew**.

Augusta   Pervert. Boy lover.

Cardew   John.

Augusta   Do I sound Irish to you? No.

She kicks **Cardew**.

Say it. No.
No more Irish pokery. No more Miss O'Flaherty.
It was a music evening. I can sing only one song and that
is in French, which I was afraid would sound suggestive.
But I took my chances. Abandoned or no, I determined to
give it my best shot.
Now, as I'm sure you can imagine, I do not have a
pleasant voice but it carries well enough. And the Jewel
Song carried all the way to Lord Bracknell. Yes, your man
Bracknell. I have him.

She kicks **Cardew**.

Oh, contain my excitement. Oh contain my tongue.
Contain my heart.

She kicks **Cardew**.

He said: 'Your voice impressed me.'
I said: 'Volume often impresses more than beauty.'
And he said: 'How true, but so few women really
appreciate volume. They spend all their time trying to
acquire more beauty when all they require is to be a little
louder.'
And so, naturally, I continued the conversation at a quite
extraordinary volume and so caught Lord Bracknell's heart.
And now I shall be Lady Bracknell and I shall have very
many children and they will all be completely English.

She kicks **Cardew** *repeatedly*.

Phil   Oh shit. Not breathing.

Augusta   Oh, Rule Britannia. Rule Britannia.

Phil   Make him breathe. Make him breathe.

Augusta   I know nothing of motherhood yet. I thought marriage first, as happens in all the best families.

Exit **Augusta**.

Phil *shakes the baby.*

Phil   Come on. Please. Come on.
(*Taking baby to* **Cardew**.) Can't you make him breathe?

Cardew   No, John. Dead to me now.

Phil *shakes the baby.*

Phil   Come on cunt. Breathe. Come on.

Phil *puts the baby down. Lights a cigarette.*

Phil   Breathe – you.

Phil *burns the baby's skin with the tip of his cigarette. It cries.*

Phil   There. See. Can breathe if you try. Good.

Enter **Constance**.

Constance   This is mine. This came from me. What it feels, I shall feel. Here. Here. To me. Give me the child.

Phil   Yes. Alright.

Constance   Oh yes. Come here. Come here. Let me feel something.

She takes the baby.

Constance   And now, of course, it should flow through me. Now I should feel overwhelmed by a mother's love.

Phil   And what do you feel?

Constance   Nothing.

Phil   Here. Give him to me.

Constance   No. It will come. Hold him long enough and it must come. Don't want to look down and see – what? – little square bundle of feet and teeth and eyes. That is not it, is it? No. No. No. Should see love. That is quite the

proper thing to see. So why? Feed him. Feed him. That
will do it. Yes. That will do it.

Enter **Moncrieff** *and* **Prism**.

Moncrieff   Oh my love. No. No. Come.

Constance   Must do my duty.

Moncrieff   Not the duty of an animal.

Constance   Must be as one with the child.

Moncrieff   Not like this. Come.
Now – hand the child over. Cling to the child and the
child will cling to you.

Constance *hands the baby to* **Prism**.

Moncrieff   Now we will go about our business. My
billiards, your piano. And from time to time the child will
be shown to us and we will be shown to the child. And so
the proper degree of affection between parent and child will
grow. You understand?

Constance   Yes.

Moncrieff   Good.

Exit **Moncrieff** *and* **Constance**.

Prism   You were born in quite the wrong family were
you not? Neither father nor mother to care for you. So,
why should I?

Prism *sits and works on her novel. Baby cries.*

Prism   I'll thank you for a moment's silence. Please. If I
could just enjoy a moment's silence.

Phil   Here. I'm good with him. I'll . . .

Phil *takes the baby.*

Prism   Well, that is a little better.
Really, how am I to deal adequately with fiction when
reality keeps making such rude interruptions on my time?
Because, really, you are a single infant. You really won't

make one bit of difference to the world.

Whereas this is a novel. Think of the emotion and instruction contained in a three-volume novel and think of the thousands of readers.

I have just reached the part where she goes into the night, out into the storm to challenge the ghost . . .

Phil Isn't breathing.

(*Taking baby to* **Prism**.) Isn't breathing.

Prism I must have peace. Peace. I don't want you. Why won't someone take you away? Why won't the bogeyman or anyone take you away?

Cardew Might I be allowed . . .

Prism Mr Cardew. I thought they had driven you from the town.

Cardew I will be leaving London shortly. I will begin again. I thought the coast. Worthing, I think. Nobody much bothers what happens in Worthing.

Prism But you will still have your boys?

Cardew If I cannot care for another what am I? But I have been too liberal with my charity, my care has been too ostentatious. Now I shall care for just one lost soul, one boy.

Prism A child in need of care? A child ignored and forgotten by its parents?

Cardew Exactly. Might I have . . . ?

Prism Bags become so easily muddled at Victoria station. It is quite possible, in a moment of mental abstraction, I should place my manuscript in the perambulator and the baby in this handbag. What a confusion. And that, similarly abstracted, you should mistake my bag for your own.

Cardew Victoria Station? Which line?

Prism The Brighton line.

Cardew   Thank you, thank you.

Exit **Cardew**.

Prism   To he who needs the child, the child shall be given. That is what justice means.

Exit **Prism**.

Phil   Oh no. Can't get me like that. Know how to make you start again. See I know how.

Phil *stubs the cigarette on the baby. Nothing.*

Phil   Come on. Come on.

Stubs the cigarette. Nothing. Again. Again. Again.

Phil   Come on. Come on.

Phil *pushes the cigarette into the baby's eyes.*

Phil   Just gonna be awkward? Just not gonna breathe eh? Alright. Alright.

Phil *sits, looks at the baby. Long pause.*

Phil *puts the baby in a bin-bag.*

Enter **Cardew** *with handbag. Sets it down carefully. Opens it. Brings out a baby.*

Cardew   My own.

Enter **Lorraine** *with shopping bag. Puts down shopping bag. Goes to cradle. Sees it is empty.*

Phil   I did a bad thing. I . . .

Lorraine *goes to bin-bag, picks it up.*

Cardew   My own one.

Lorraine *cradles the bin-bag.* **Cardew** *cradles the baby.* **Phil** *howls.*

End.

A SELECTED LIST OF
METHUEN MODERN PLAYS

☐	CLOSER	Patrick Marber	£6.99
☐	THE BEAUTY QUEEN OF LEENANE	Martin McDonagh	£6.99
☐	A SKULL IN CONNEMARA	Martin McDonagh	£6.99
☐	THE LONESOME WEST	Martin McDonagh	£6.99
☐	THE CRIPPLE OF INISHMAAN	Martin McDonagh	£6.99
☐	THE STEWARD OF CHRISTENDOM	Sebastian Barry	£6.99
☐	SHOPPING AND F***ING	Mark Ravenhill	£6.99
☐	FAUST (FAUST IS DEAD)	Mark Ravenhill	£5.99
☐	POLYGRAPH	Robert Lepage and Marie Brassard	£6.99
☐	BEAUTIFUL THING	Jonathan Harvey	£6.99
☐	MEMORY OF WATER & FIVE KINDS OF SILENCE	Shelagh Stephenson	£7.99
☐	WISHBONES	Lucinda Coxon	£6.99
☐	BONDAGERS & THE STRAW CHAIR	Sue Glover	£9.99
☐	SOME VOICES & PALE HORSE	Joe Penhall	£7.99
☐	KNIVES IN HENS	David Harrower	£6.99
☐	BOYS' LIFE & SEARCH AND DESTROY	Howard Korder	£8.99
☐	THE LIGHTS	Howard Korder	£6.99
☐	SERVING IT UP & A WEEK WITH TONY	David Eldridge	£8.99
☐	INSIDE TRADING	Malcolm Bradbury	£6.99
☐	MASTERCLASS	Terrence McNally	£5.99
☐	EUROPE & THE ARCHITECT	David Grieg	£7.99
☐	BLUE MURDER	Peter Nichols	£6.99
☐	BLASTED & PHAEDRA'S LOVE	Sarah Kane	£7.99

• All Methuen Drama books are available through mail order or from your local bookshop.

Please send cheque/eurocheque/postal order (sterling only) Access, Visa, Mastercard, Diners Card, Switch or Amex.

☐☐☐☐☐☐☐☐☐☐☐☐☐☐☐☐

Expiry Date:_____Signature: _____

Please allow 75 pence per book for post and packing U.K.
Overseas customers please allow £1.00 per copy for post and packing.

ALL ORDERS TO:

Methuen Books, Books by Post, TBS Limited, The Book Service, Colchester Road, Frating Green, Colchester, Essex CO7 7DW.

NAME: _____

ADDRESS: _____

_____

_____

Please allow 28 days for delivery. Please tick box if you do not wish to receive any additional information ☐

Prices and availability subject to change without notice.

METHUEN SCREENPLAYS

☐ BEAUTIFUL THING	Jonathan Harvey	£6.99
☐ THE ENGLISH PATIENT	Anthony Minghella	£7.99
☐ THE CRUCIBLE	Arthur Miller	£6.99
☐ THE WIND IN THE WILLOWS	Terry Jones	£7.99
☐ PERSUASION	Jane Austen, adapted by Nick Dear	£6.99
☐ TWELFTH NIGHT	Shakespeare, adapted by Trevor Nunn	£7.99
☐ THE KRAYS	Philip Ridley	£7.99
☐ THE AMERICAN DREAMS (THE REFLECTING SKIN & THE PASSION OF DARKLY NOON)	Philip Ridley	£8.99
☐ MRS BROWN	Jeremy Brock	£7.99
☐ THE GAMBLER	Dostoyevsky, adapted by Nick Dear	£7.99
☐ TROJAN EDDIE	Billy Roche	£7.99
☐ THE WINGS OF THE DOVE	Hossein Amini	£7.99
☐ THE ACID HOUSE TRILOGY	Irvine Welsh	£8.99
☐ THE LONG GOOD FRIDAY	Barrie Keeffe	£6.99
☐ SLING BLADE	Billy Bob Thornton	£7.99

• All Methuen Drama books are available through mail order or from your local bookshop.

Please send cheque/eurocheque/postal order (sterling only) Access, Visa, Mastercard, Diners Card, Switch or Amex.

☐☐☐☐☐☐☐☐☐☐☐☐☐☐☐☐

Expiry Date:_____ Signature: _____

Please allow 75 pence per book for post and packing U.K.
Overseas customers please allow £1.00 per copy for post and packing.

ALL ORDERS TO:

Methuen Books, Books by Post, TBS Limited, The Book Service, Colchester Road, Frating Green, Colchester, Essex CO7 7DW.

NAME: _____

ADDRESS: _____

_____

_____

Please allow 28 days for delivery. Please tick box if you do not wish to receive any additional information ☐

Prices and availability subject to change without notice.

METHUEN DRAMA
MONOLOGUE & SCENE BOOKS

☐ CONTEMPORARY SCENES FOR ACTORS (MEN)	Earley and Keil	£8.99
☐ CONTEMPORARY SCENES FOR ACTORS (WOMEN)	Earley and Keil	£8.99
☐ THE CLASSICAL MONOLOGUE (MEN)	Earley and Keil	£7.99
☐ THE CLASSICAL MONOLOGUE (WOMEN)	Earley and Keil	£7.99
☐ THE CONTEMPORARY MONOLOGUE (MEN)	Earley and Keil	£7.99
☐ THE CONTEMPORARY MONOLOGUE (WOMEN)	Earley and Keil	£7.99
☐ THE MODERN MONOLOGUE (MEN)	Earley and Keil	£7.99
☐ THE MODERN MONOLOGUE (WOMEN)	Earley and Keil	£7.99
☐ THE METHUEN AUDITION BOOK FOR MEN	Annika Bluhm	£6.99
☐ THE METHUEN AUDITION BOOK FOR WOMEN	Annika Bluhm	£6.99
☐ THE METHUEN AUDITION BOOK FOR YOUNG ACTORS	Anne Harvey	£6.99
☐ THE METHUEN BOOK OF DUOLOGUES FOR YOUNG ACTORS	Anne Harvey	£6.99

• All Methuen Drama books are available through mail order or from your local bookshop.

Please send cheque/eurocheque/postal order (sterling only) Access, Visa, Mastercard, Diners Card, Switch or Amex.

☐☐☐☐☐☐☐☐☐☐☐☐☐☐☐

Expiry Date:_____ Signature: _____

Please allow 75 pence per book for post and packing U.K.
Overseas customers please allow £1.00 per copy for post and packing.

ALL ORDERS TO:

Methuen Books, Books by Post, TBS Limited, The Book Service, Colchester Road, Frating Green, Colchester, Essex CO7 7DW.

NAME: _____

ADDRESS: _____

_____

Please allow 28 days for delivery. Please tick box if you do not wish to receive any additional information   ☐

Prices and availability subject to change without notice.

Methuen World Classics
include

Jean Anouilh (two volumes)
John Arden (two volumes)
Arden & D'Arcy
Brendan Behan
Aphra Behn
Bertolt Brecht (six volumes)
Büchner
Bulgakov
Calderón
Anton Chekhov
Noël Coward (five volumes)
Eduardo De Filippo
Max Frisch
Gorky
Harley Granville Barker
    (two volumes)
Henrik Ibsen (six volumes)
Lorca (three volumes)
Marivaux

Mustapha Matura
David Mercer (two volumes)
Arthur Miller (five volumes)
Molière
Musset
Clifford Odets
Joe Orton
A. W. Pinero
Luigi Pirandello
Terence Rattigan
W. Somerset Maugham
    (two volumes)
Wole Soyinka
August Strindberg
    (three volumes)
J. M. Synge
Ramón del Valle-Inclán
Frank Wedekind
Oscar Wilde

For a Complete Catalogue of Methuen Drama titles
write to:

Methuen Drama
20 Vauxhall Bridge Road
London SW1V 2SA